Full Score

SEE SAW SWING

FOR VIOLIN:
METATECHNICAL EXERCISES VOLUME 1

Fundamentals to improve tone, technique,
note reading, rhythm, ensemble, and intonation
while accelerating progress for beginning
and remedial violin students

Michael Alexander Strauss

If I can stop one Heart from breaking
I shall not live in vain
If I can ease one Life the Aching
Or cool one Pain

Or help one fainting Robin
Unto his Nest again
I shall not live in Vain.

Emily Dickinson

Thank you to my teachers:

Joseph Primavera
Alice Lindsay
Thomas Lindsay
Lucy Parker
Al Filosa
Eugene Lehner
Paul Doktor
George Neikrug
Dorothee Metlitzkee
Raphael Hillyer
Scott Nickrenz
Heidi Castleman
Benjamin Zander
Karen Tuttle
Marjorie Barstow

Cover design and artwork by
Maggie.Grundy@gmail.com

See   saw   see   saw   will   you   be   my   friend?

HOW TO USE SEE SAW SWING

These FUNDAMENTAL exercises are an experiment designed to accelerate learning for beginning and remedial students, with positive results in improving tone, technique, shifting, double stops, ensemble playing, and rhythm.

See Saw Swing is based on Whole Brain Learning. Every measure "swings" the student from the left hemisphere of the brain to the right as they alternate string crossings with fingered patterns. This alternation from side to side strengthens the Corpus Callosum- the nerve network that divides and connects the hemispheres- leading to progress that students describe as being "magical."

Scientifically, to reproduce the results of an experiment, it is necessary to replicate as much as possible every aspect of the experiment. Obviously, because all teachers are unique, this is impossible. However, it is possible to use See Saw Swing exercises as I have learned to use them: when I wrote this book, in 2006, I had no idea what I had created and didn't know how to use it. But after fourteen years of practice, combined with research on brain activity, I now have an algorithm that every teacher is free to employ.

With young students, sing the tune with the prescribed words. Always show them how to differentiate between long strokes and short strokes, and to practice the exercises in different parts of the bow. Also be certain to teach that each string has a different weight, and every time you shorten a string by stopping it, it weighs less.

See Saw Swing is built on the principle of repetition, with two notes changing in every line ("Musical Phonics"). Also, the various finger patterns and rhythmic applications are geared to mastering different pieces of music. Because it is easy for the student to learn to play the first pages, it is crucial to have them practice at least two pages at a time; the goal is to physically condition the student to play the instrument.

HYPOTHESIS: ANY STUDENT WHO CAN PLAY EVERY EXERCISE IN THIS BOOK IS READY TO LEARN MUSIC AT THE LEVEL OF THE VIVALDI CONCERTO IN A MINOR.

These 60 pages, learned at the rate of one per week, will take 60 weeks.
Fourteen months from Twinkle to Vivaldi. Learned at the average of 4 pages per week? 15 weeks. And I've done that with students, again and again.

10

See　Saw　See　Saw　Yes　I'll　be　your　friend.

THE ALGORITHM

1. ASAP have the student practice at least two pages nonstop (within four weeks).

2. ASAP practice D Major and G major sections.

3. In the first month, train student to play fingered measures vertically. One note changes per line. This is "Musical Phonics." (PARADIGM SHIFT).

4. Play the exercises in canon with your student within the first four weeks.

5. The sooner you introduce Bb, Eb, and Ab major, the easier your student will make the adjustment. *See Saw Swing* is a paradigm shift in violin training that operates on the principle of immersion.

6. It is preferable to introduce the 4th finger using a Bb major pattern, because it is only a half step.

7. Within eight weeks of lessons, combined with musical pieces, the student can feel comfortable alternating A Major and Bb Major. At this point, pencil in natural signs in A Major (etc.) to turn the A Major scale into a Mixolydian scale (Low 2nd on the E,but high second on the A string); this conditions the student to easily negotiate the low second fingers of Bach Minuets (8-12 weeks).

8. As soon as the student is comfortable switching between A Major and Bb Major, take them to B Major and the 1st finger bridge. This trains the high 3rd finger (10-14 weeks).

9. Pencil in slurs within the first 8 weeks of study. The longer you wait to teach slurring, the more difficult it becomes to learn (PARADIGM SHIFT).

10. Introduce the rhythm pages within the first four weeks. Not only should you have them apply the rhythms to the exercises, but practice the rhythm pages in canon, which creates a steady quarter note beat (PARADIGM SHIFT).

11. At this point, your student is ready to skip to the final chapter, Vocalization, and learn the See Saw melody in ascending half steps. The earlier you start your beginner on shifting, the more easily and freely the child will take to it (PARADIGM SHIFT!).

12. The hooked bowing exercises prove to be difficult for most students. Differentiate the long stroke (arm) from the short stroke (wrist).

13 The double string crossing section is an advanced exercise which prepares the student to learn the Bach Double Concerto and other difficult string crossing pieces. Take it slow, but get to it within the first five months of study.

14. Within three months, students should be practicing eight pages per day nonstop and accelerating the tempo. Always alternate exercise practice with perfecting their new music.

15. Practice in canon frequently to improve listening, rhythm and ensemble skills..

16. TheVocalization exercises, which use all the fingers, are crucial for ear training. You will find that mastery of half step shifts -which mimic a voice student's vocalization exercises- make it easy for the student to shift from first to third position (PARADIGM SHIFT!).

17.The Lydian Tetrachord exercise helps develop flexibility in the fingers.

18. The E Major page near the end of the book introduces shifting between different positions. Once your students feel comfortable, have them go back to the beginning of the book and practice *See Saw Swing* exercises in different positions.

19. Within the first six months, have your students practice the final page, Double Stops. Then, apply double stop practice to every exercise.

20. When your students are able to negotiate every exercise in this book, even if they are still learning music at the level of Suzuki Volume 2, they will be ready to learn anything at the level of Suzuki Volume 4. I have had remedial students make the leap after three months of lessons. Beginners aged 9 and over can attain this in six months (PARADIGM SHIFT!!!).

WHOLE BRAIN LEARNING

To paraphrase a direction from a popular beginning violin book:
Learn to play by perfecting one skill at a time. Do not go onto the next step until you have command over this one.

It sounds so simple, and seems so correct, but is that how any child learned to walk, talk, socialize, read, or hit a baseball? Did you master one phoneme at a time, never going on to the next sound until you had command over this one?

I don't think so.

And yet it sounds so correct to practice one step at a time, and here is why: **This is precisely how the left hemisphere of the brain processes data.**

There is a time and place for the linear perfectionism practiced by the left hemisphere but not at the beginning stages of violin study and especially not for children.

The first five lines of *See Saw Swing* includes all the notes of a major scale, three rhythmic values, and many string crossings. I have had students work through the first 20 pages of *See Saw Swing* in less than three months and then be promoted out of their beginner string class in school (4th grade) to join the 5th grade orchestra, laughing all the way because it was easy!

How? By activating whole brain learning. *See Saw Swing* students find their way around their instruments the same way that they learned to walk, talk, count, and read: a joyfully childish blend of exploration without fear of failing.

When they get both hemispheres of their brain in the room at the same time, they become so much smarter!

***See Saw Swing* does this by oscillating students' attention-processing from one hemisphere to the other, generating an accelerated learning curve. In this system, using exercises bypasses students' debilitating habits and effects dynamic changes at the neuroplastic level. Whole brain learning also lights up childrens' forebrains, freeing them to apply critical thinking to their elementary learning challenges.**

So, as your embark on your personal experiments with *See Saw Swing,* please think like a scientist and take the challenge of replicating my experimental results.

Michael Alexander Strauss
January 29, 2020

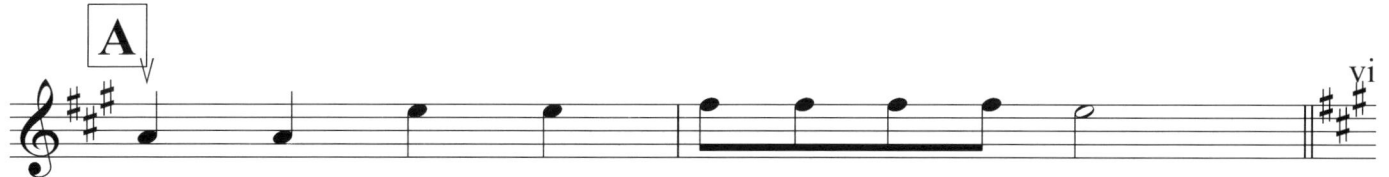

TABLE OF CONTENTS

SEE SAW SWING

LONG STROKES, SHORT STROKES, STRING CROSSINGS

WE LEARN BY DOING EXERCISES.

A MAJOR

Be sure to use long strokes for the quarter notes, and very short, for the eighths.

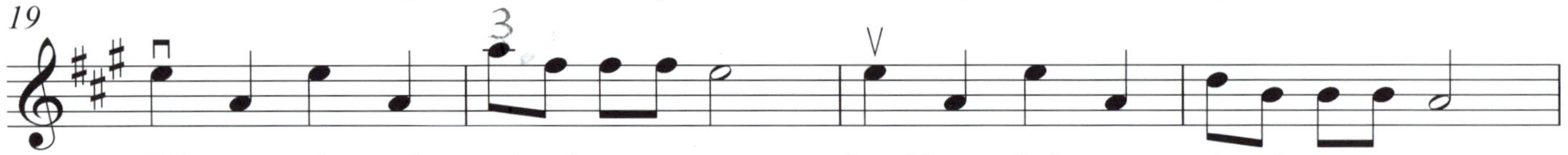

When crossing strings, take time to rotate your shoulder and change arm level.

Canonic entrance.

Canonic entrance.

Canonic entrance.

47

Obviously, practice at different parts of the bow and different tempi.

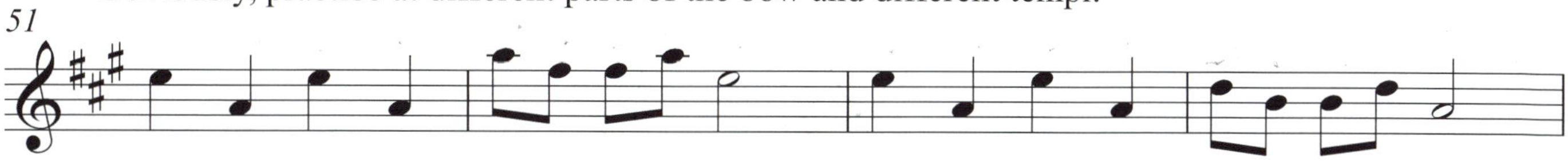

51

And vary the dynamics!!

55

Remember to practice in canon to develop ensemble skills.

59

63

67

71

75

79

83

3

REDIRECT PAGE

GO TO PAGES 7-8 AND PRACTICE THE SYMMETRICAL REPEAT ON THE A & D STRINGS.`.

NOW ALSO BEGIN CANONIC PRACTICE IN LESSONS.

GO TO PAGES 11-12 AND PRACTICE THE SYMMETRICAL REPEAT ON THE D & G STRINGS.`

GO TO PAGES 19-21 AND PRACTICE LOW 1ST, 2ND & 4TH FINGERS, ETC.

METATECHNICAL SUPPORT

1. When your student can play the first 5 lines of See Saw Swing in A Major they will easily learn to play and read Twinkle.

2. It is a metatechnical principle that the longer that beginners only play on the E/A string nexus, the more difficult it becomes for them to "find the bead" on the other two string pairs.

3. The "Bead" is a quick way to describe "Spot/Bite/Speed" (contact point, friction, and bow speed).

4. Heavier strings require a stronger bead (Call it whatever you like; at the metalevel, semantic conficts do not exist).

5. The longer that beginners only play with the 0 1 2 3/ 1 step, 1 step, 1/2 step pattern, the more difficult it becomes to learn other patterns.

6. Therefore, as quickly as possible, move the student to the 1 2 3 4 Bb Major Scale pattern (within four weeks of lessons is not unreasonable).

7. Also, metatechnically, it is less stressful for beginners to use the 4th finger on a half step.

8. After beginners become comfortable with the 4th finger half step, return to the second half of A Major, D major, and G major sections to practice the extended 4th finger.

9. Train your students to alternate practice between new music and familiar fundamental exercises.

10. Perfectionism is the enemy of progress, the destroyer of emotional balance, the killer of joy.

11. "All together, one step at a time." F. M. Alexander.   This aphorism is the epitome of whole brain learning. It is nonlinear, which means that the left hemisphere of the brain, which is either a square or a demented rectangle, cannot process it.

12. The right hemisphere is oceanic. Practice these fundamental exercises as if they were MUSIC.

5

Here is the whole step (extended) fourth finger.

And here, too.

D MAJOR

Now employ higher arm levels for the bow and the left arm swung slightly to the right.

As you gain mastery, speed up the tempo.

9

G MAJOR

When one person starts at the beginning, and the
second at the end, See Saw Swings becomes a Crab Canon!

Practice backwards, playing from right to left.

On this final page of G, D and A major scale patterns, I have suggested bowings.

14

REDIRECT

Go to pages 28 etc. to practice the 1st finger bridge and high 3rd finger.

Return to the opening 12 pages and add naturals (low 2nd finger) only to the second measures. This creates a Mixolydian Scale and prepares the beginner to learn Bach Minuets.

REMEMBER: CANONIC PRACTICE AS OFTEN AS POSSIBLE!!

Go to Page 64 and practice in chords.

Go to Rhythm Pages and practice them in unison and in canon with your students.

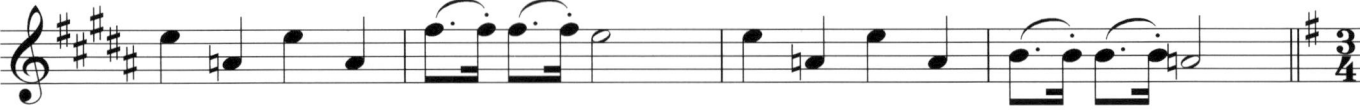

METATECHNICAL SUPPORT

1. Once your students can play mixolydian scales, they will easily master the Bach minuets.

2. See Saw Swing is nothing but fundamentals presented with binary logic.

3. The exercises are built on making binary choices at every step of technical development. From the first measures, students learn to differentiate one string from another, one finger from another, one rhythm from another.

4. Accelerated development depends on introducing as many different fingering and rhythmic choices as quickly as possible. The left hemisphere of the brain, which is square and limited, cannot possibly process this revolutionary idea. But the right hemisphere of the brain, in balance with the left, is where music, learning and "talent" happen.

5. When a student gets bored with repetitions in A Major, add accidentals, add slurs, have them practice with various rhythms, practice as chords, and show them how to use a stop watch.

6. Time a student playing an entire page. Suppose it takes 75 seconds. Now, time it again, but ask them to bring it in as close as possible to 60 seconds.

7. Of course, it is possible to work out metronome rates for every possible timing, and there is a time for that, but kids really love the game of aiming for a precise time without using the metronome.

8. Practicing with the first finger bridge prepares the left hand for advanced left hand techniques. Also, learning the first finger bridge compels students to face their fingernails forward. Furthermore, for tuning, students can learn to fine tune by altering the pressure on each string. As you press down harder, you can raise a pitch by 10 cents.

9. Be certain to have students alternate between the different finger patterns. Again, the key to accelerated progress (beautiful bowing/tone, excellent intonation, easy note reading, shifting, vibrato, velocity and more) is that **EVERYTHING FITS TOGETHER.**

10. Do not get stuck on any single pattern. Do switch frequently between practicing exercises and learning new music. Do not be surprised when beginners master Suzuki Volume 1 in six months or less. Do not be surprised when they learn Volume 2 songs two to three each week. And do not be surprised when your beginner is ready to leap to the Vivaldi a minor concerto in one year or less.

RHYTHMIC VARIATIONS

These variations become increasingly more complex. Many are not for beginners, but by the time the beginner has reached the end of the book, he/she should be attempting all of them.

I have found the most effective way to introduce these rhythms is to practice them in order on these two pages. Only then should they be transferred to the other iterations of "See Saw Swings."

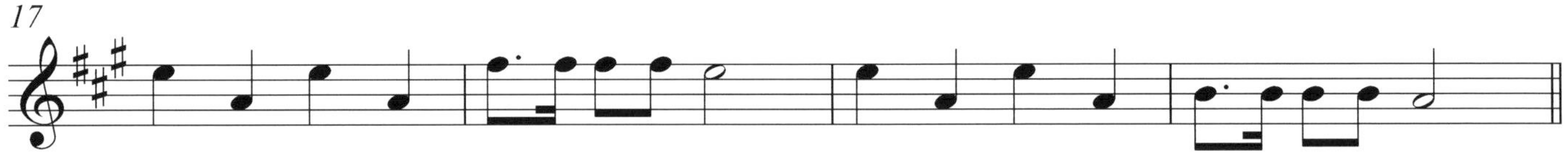

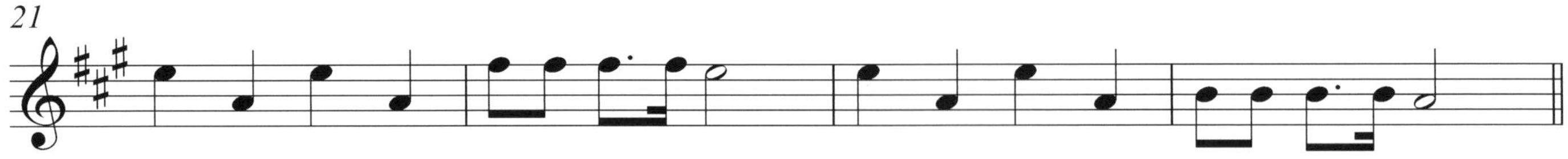

LOW FIRST, SECOND, AND FOURTH FINGERS

A MAJOR/Bb MAJOR

69

Here we introduce the low 1st finger.

73

There is now a large space (major 3rd) between the 1st & 3rd fingers.

77

81

85

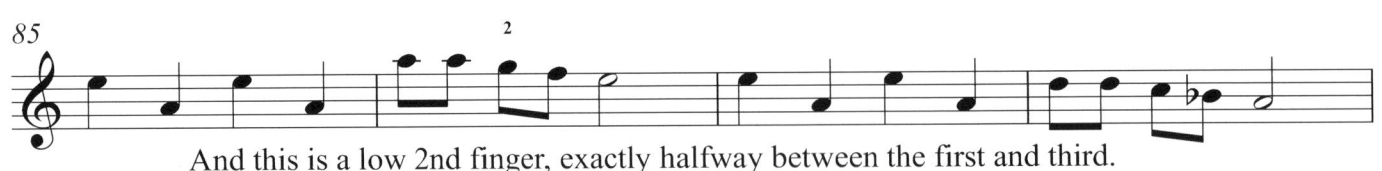

And this is a low 2nd finger, exactly halfway between the first and third.

89

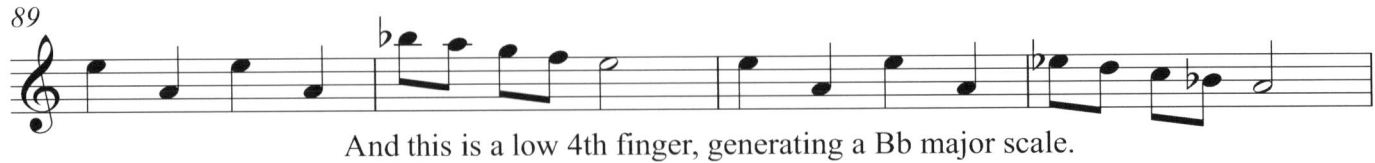

And this is a low 4th finger, generating a Bb major scale.

93

These iterations are polytonal. In fact, in *See Saw Swing* the beginner is introduced to scales in all 12 major keys.

D MAJOR/Eb MAJOR

Leave out the open strings and your are playing an Eb Major Scale.

G MAJOR/Ab MAJOR

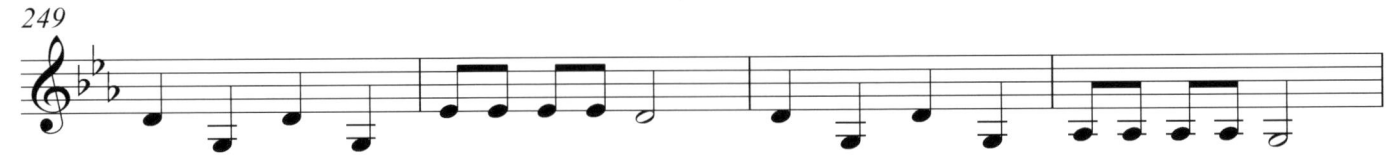

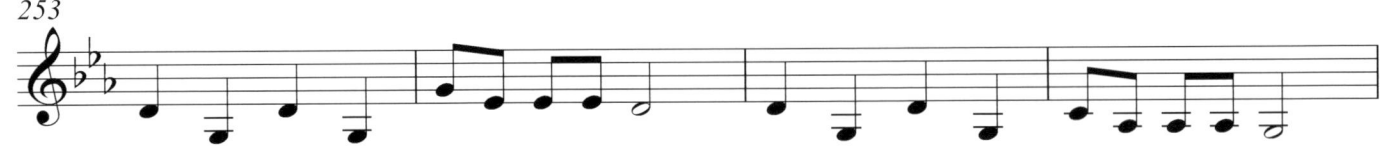

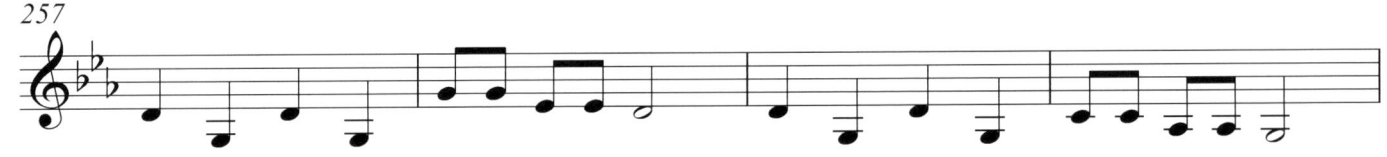

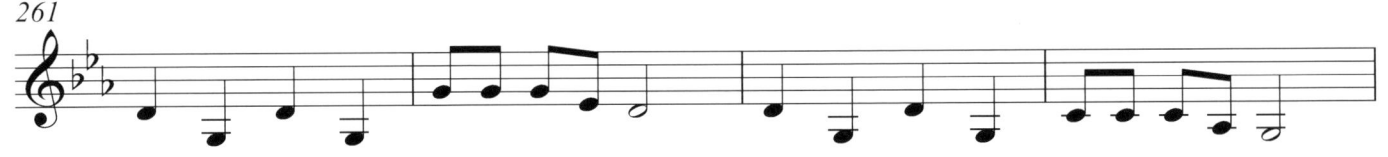

Leave out the open strings and your are playing an Ab Major Scale.

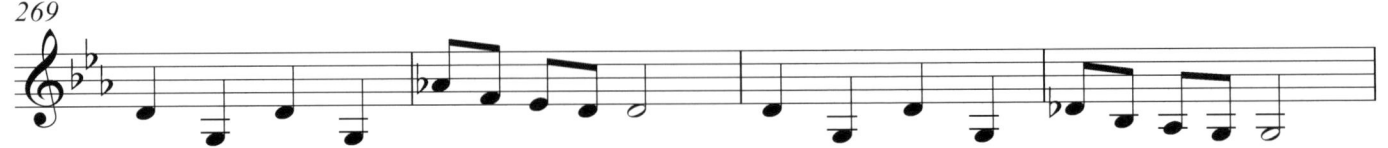

273

277

281

285

289

293

297

FIRST FINGER BRIDGE/ HIGH THIRD FINGER

B MAJOR

Keep first finger down across both strings.

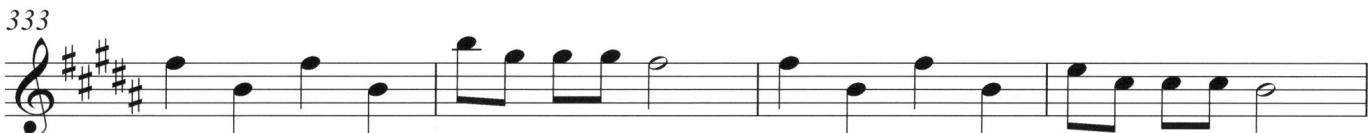

Keep the first finger down across both strings at all times!!

In this exercise, the first finger never moves! Ever!

Here is a high 3rd finger!

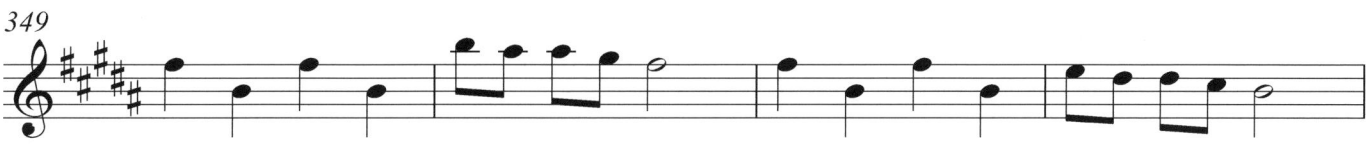

B Major Scale.

E MAJOR

E Major Scale.

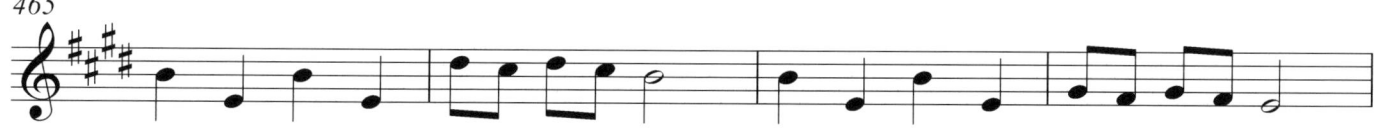

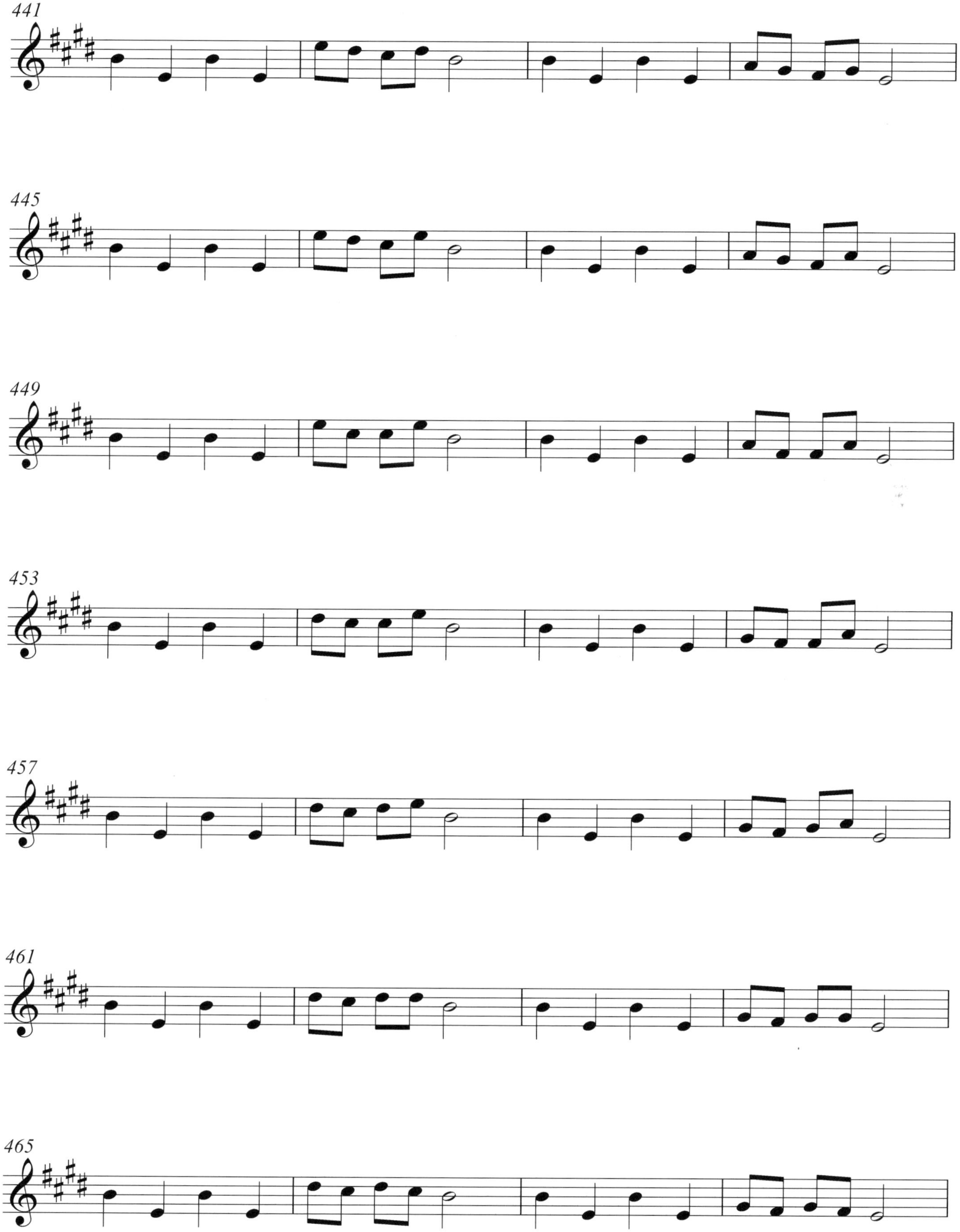
441
445
449
453
457
461
465

A MAJOR

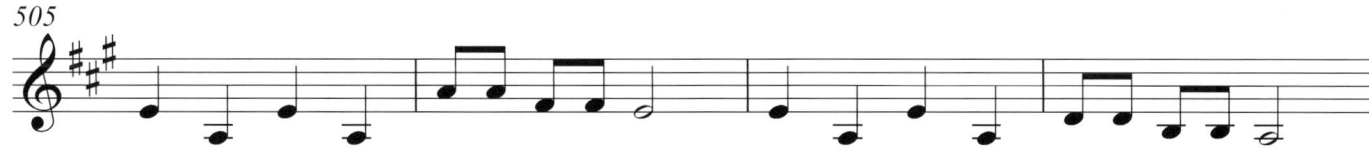

A Major Scale on G and D strings.

REDIRECT

Go to page 55 and practice shifting/vocalization.

Go to page 46 for Lydian tetrachords and the second finger bridge.

METATECHNICAL SUPPORT

Excerpt from Gavotte by Lully, with 3rd position

1. The Metatechnical principle holds that the longer the student waits to learn to shift and play in positions, the more difficult it will be to learn.

2. Vocalization means that students learn to climb a string the way a voice student learns to gradually develop their high notes. As the string shortens, it tightens and becomes lighter. The lighter string demands a lighter bead (spot/bite/speed).

3. Because the vocalization exercise is gradual, students teach themselves to find the bead without difficulty. The half step shifts also prepare the student to shift up and down from 1st to 3rd positions.

4. The vocalization exercises become increasingly complex. When students add all fingers, they learn to narrow the spaces between their fingers as they climb the strings.

5. The next exercise intoduces arpeggios and major scales played quickly under a single slur.

6. The final vocalization exercise focuses on chromatic changes.

7. All the vocalization exercises demand that students use their ear to search for pitch. You will discover that after trying vocalization, when the student returns to 1st position, regardless of the intervals, they will play with greater confidence and accuracy.

8. A Lydian Tetrachord has three whole steps; every major scale can be divided into a major trichord separated by a half step from the Lydian Tetrachord. It is the final element in the most common finger patterns: Major trichord, Minor trichord, and Lydian Tetrachord.

HOOKED BOWS, RHYTHMS, AND THE LOW FIRST FINGER BRIDGE

Bb MAJOR

Keep the first finger low
across both strings.

Half position.

Always remember to practice fingered bars in columns.

Try these various articulations.

Bb Major Scale

Eb MAJOR

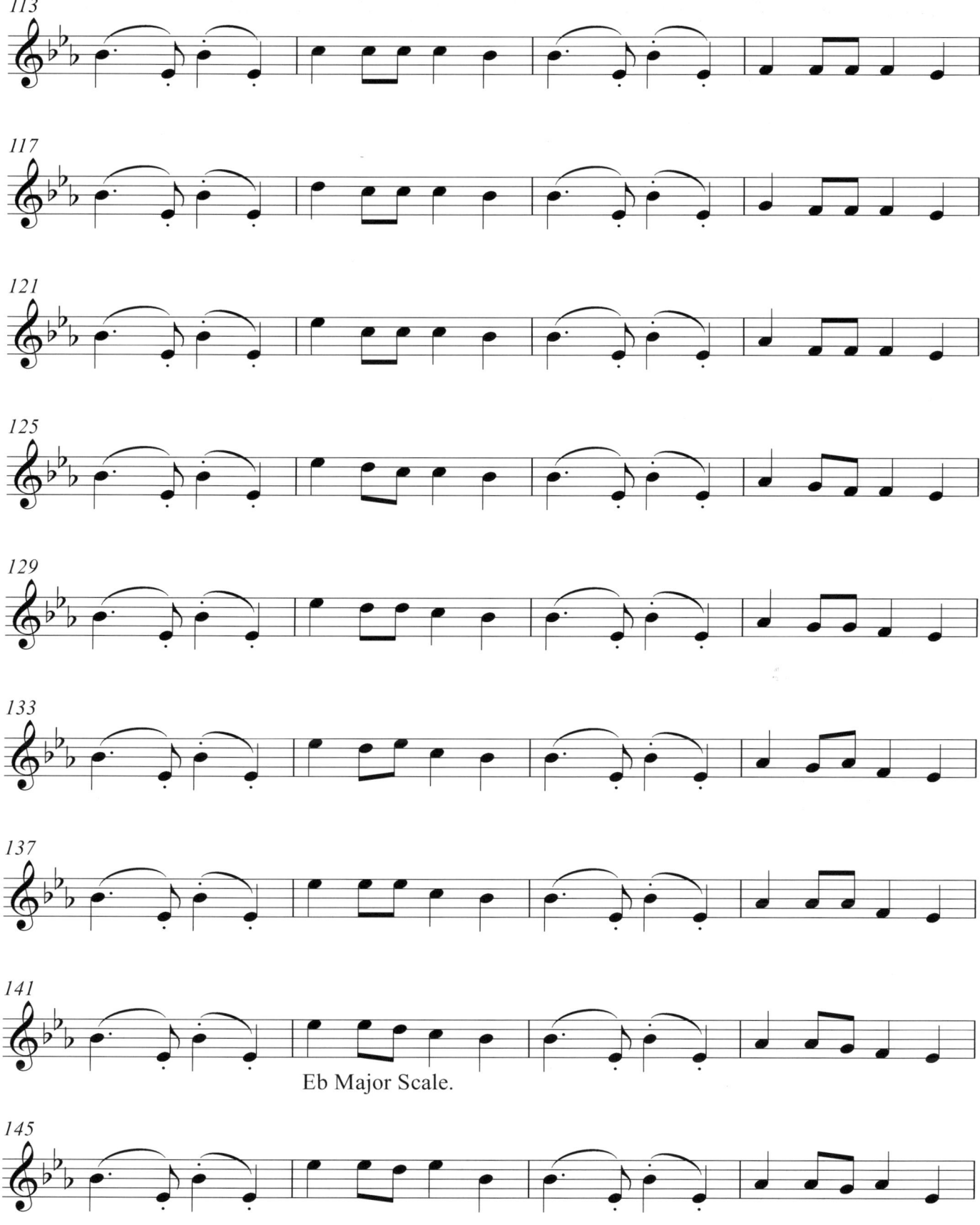

Eb Major Scale.

Ab MAJOR

Ab Major Scale.

SECOND FINGER BRIDGE/TRIPLETS/LYDIAN TETRACHORDS

Be sure to keep your second finger across both strings on all the half notes.

Use whole bows on the half notes, with a lot of expression.

3 whole steps form a Lydian tetrachord.

Be sure to metronome the triplets to keep them accurate.

As you cross strings, pay close attention to friction, bowspeed and contact point.
When friction, bowspeed and contact point are just right, that is called finding the "bead."

As the string thickens, it requires more friction and slower bowspeed, or...

...to keep the "bead", move slightly away from the bridge.

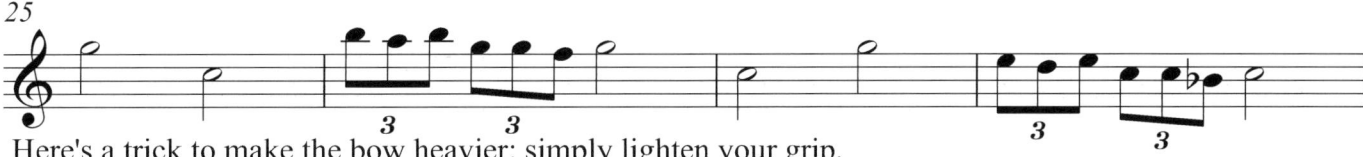

Here's a trick to make the bow heavier: simply lighten your grip.

To lighten the bow, tighten your grip!!

If you use whole bows, the triplets will alternate frog and tip; be sure tip and frog sound identical.

For these quick triplets, keep your arm quiet and have flexible fingers and wrist.

Of course, at any time, write in your own bowings. Here are examples.

REDIRECT

Go to page 39 for hooked bows and a rhythmic variation

Go to page 51 for double string crossings and quick string crossings.

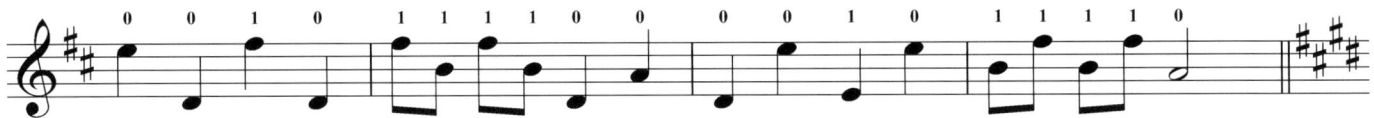

Go to page 67 for See Saw in E Major on the E string.

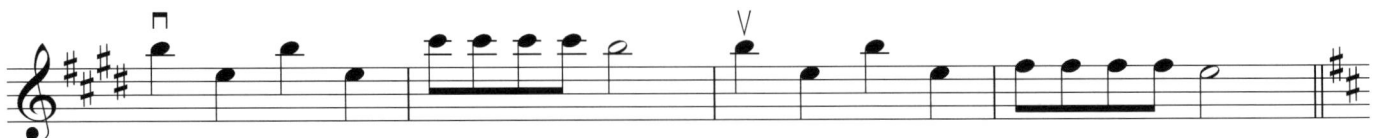

METATECHNICAL SUPPORT

Seitz Concerto in D   Your student is now able to learn this piece.

1. If you have been following the Redirect Pages, your students are now practicing the hooked bow string crossing exercise and the double string crossing exercise. For most students, these two exercises are more difficult to explore than Vocalizations.

2. Digression: Vocalization, as an approach to shifting and ear training, is a paradigm shift. They are finding their way up and down the fingerboard playing a familiar tune in different keys and positions, AND IT IS NO BIG DEAL.

3. The hooked bow exercise needs to be practiced slowly, differentiating between a long stroke for the dotted quarter note (arm), followed by a short stroke for the staccato eighth note (finger stroke). Read in *Metatechnical Systems* for a detailed exploration of balancing muscles so that the short stroke does not overtax the flexors and extensors found in the forearm.

4. Also, in the 2nd and 4th measures, use short strokes for the eighth notes and long strokes for the quarter notes.

5. At the Metalevel -the bird's eye view of the landscape of how to play the instrument- staccato strokes that begin with accents are not for beginners. PARADIGM SHIFT: it is easier to teach beginners to play beautiful tones with legato bow changes. Why? Because there is more muscular and nervous activity needed to create accents and detachment.

6. The double string crossing exercise is also a technical challenge. It requires a coordination between the shoulder (whole arm movement) and the wrist (delicate finger movement). *Metatechnical Systems* presents an exegesis on differentiating between long strokes and short strokes, and then the complications of COMPOUND STROKES, where arm and wrist motions combine in a plethora of virtuosic complications.

7. The See Saw page in E Major is the logical next step after exploring the vocalization exercises. Students then should practice every page in different positions, preferably working out fingerings for themselves.

8. If they have been diligently increasing velocity in their exercising, then they will be ready to study the Vivaldi Concerto in a minor.

DOUBLE STOP PREP
DOUBLE STRING CROSSINGS/EIGHTH NOTE CROSSINGS

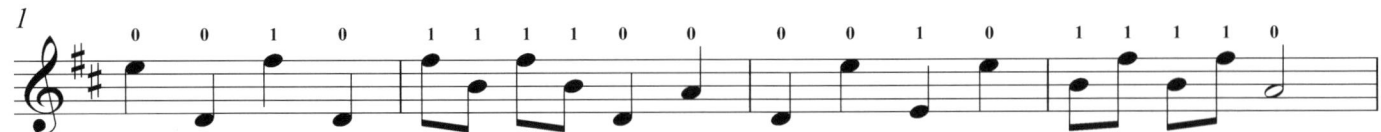

Use the whole arm and some wrist for quarter note crossings.
Use only the wrist for eighth note crossings.

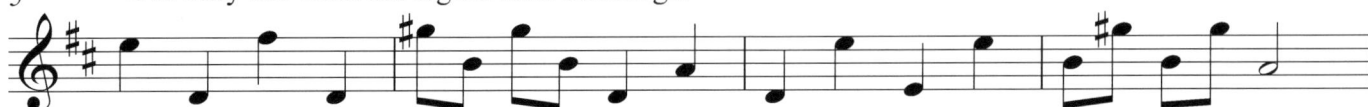

Keep both fingers down when crossing strings.

Keeping both fingers down is preparation for playing double stops.

So, also practice the eighth notes as double stops.

VOCALIZATION
INTRODUCTION TO SHIFTING AND POSITIONS

In this introduction to positions, maintain a whole step between 1st & 2nd fingers.
Maintain the 1st finger bridge always.

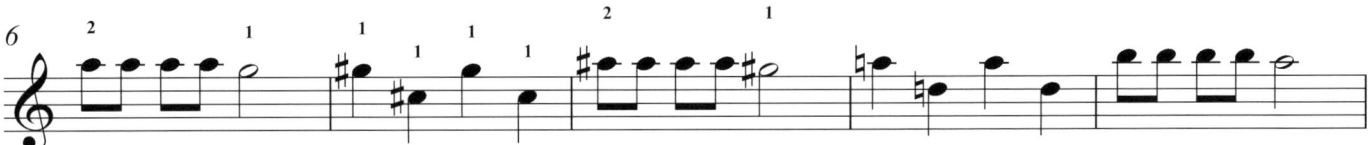

As you shorten the string, pull your two fingers closer together, ever so slightly, to stay in tune.

Use your ear and play as if you were singing. Be sure to lighten the bead as you climb.

Try leading every shift with the thumb moving first.   Keep left hand in place!!

Now, reverse the string crossing and play the quick notes on the lower string.

By now, you get the idea; always slide your whole hand up a half step.

As you climb your strings, the spacing between fingers decreases symmetrically.

Be certain to read the music as you play, to train yourself to play in these different positions.

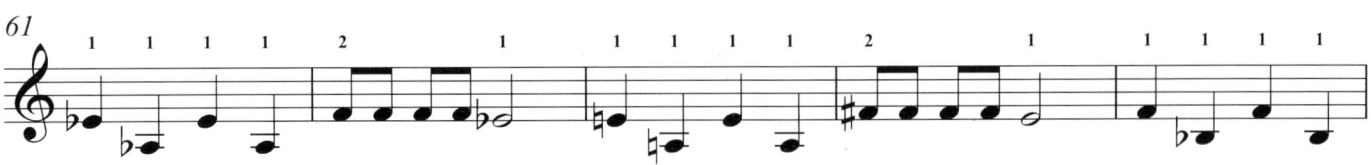

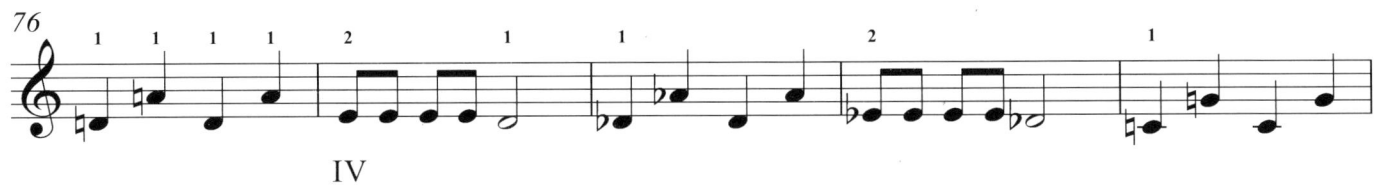

Always keep the first finger down across both strings!

Enharmonic change: B# sounds the same as C natural.

C Double Sharp sounds like D natural.

ARPEGGIOS AND ONE OCTAVE SCALES

Maintain a double first finger across both strings
while playing these scales.

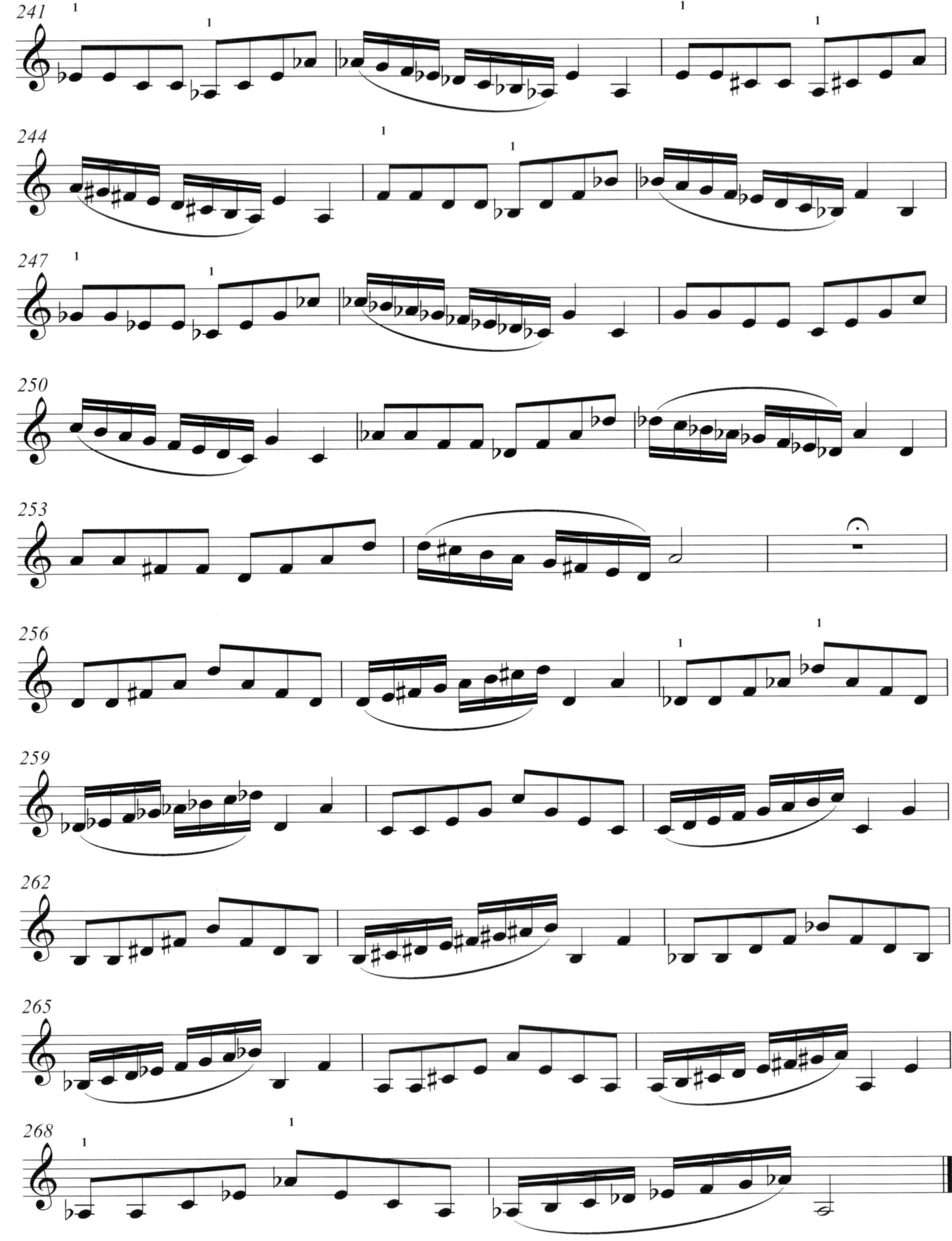

CHROMATICISM

ossia fingering

A String!

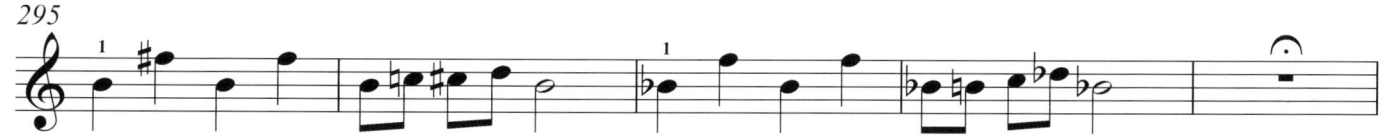

65

ossia fingering

D String!

330

335

340

345

CONGRATULATIONS! Since you have gotten this far and can play every exercise comfortably, you are ready to learn the first movement of the Seitz Concerto in D Major!

350

Now return to the beginning of the book and practice Spring Showers (et cetera) in 3rd position and then 4th posiition. Then create combinations of positions until you're comfortable reading notes with different fingerings.

355
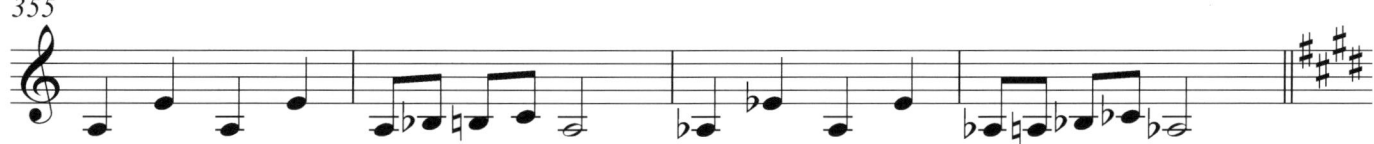

A PAGE IN 3RD AND 4TH POSITION, SHIFTING TO 1ST
E Major

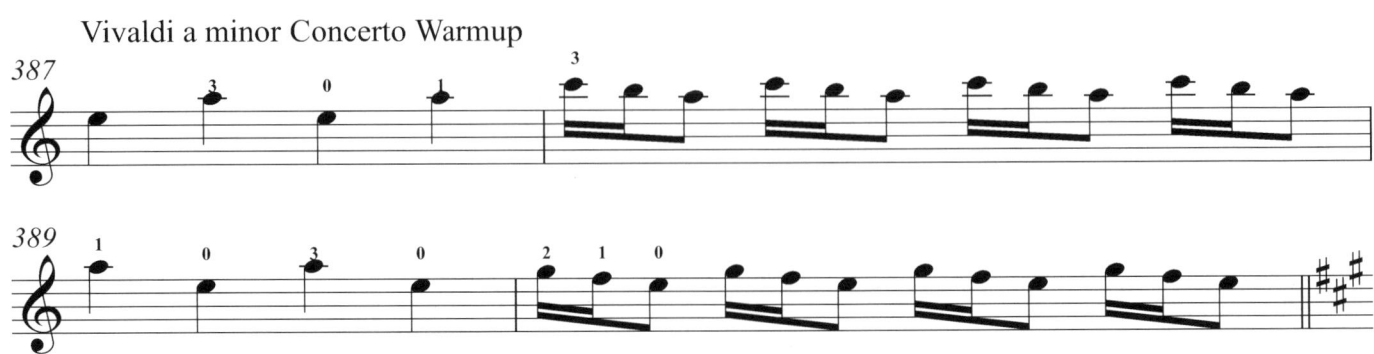

CREATE SIMILAR FINGERINGS FREELY THROUGHOUT.

Vivaldi a minor Concerto Warmup

DOUBLE STOP SUGGESTIONS

SIMILE AD LIBITUM THROUGHOUT THE BOOK.

Made in the USA
Columbia, SC
25 February 2020